The Peep & Squeak Easy-to-Read Password Assistance Book

(with tabs)

By Susan Trott

A-B
C-D
E-F
G-H
I-J
K-L
M-N
O-P
Q-R
S-T
U-V
W-X
Y-Z
0-9

ISBN 13: 978-1-998107-08-7

A

Website	
Username	
Email	
Password	
Security	
Website	
Username	
Email	
Password	
Security	
Website	
Username	
Email	
Password	
Security	

A

Website	
Username	
Email	
Password	
Security	
Website	
Username	
Email	
Password	
Security	
Website	
Username	
Email	
Password	
Security	

A

Website	
Username	
Email	
Password	
Security	
Website	
Username	
Email	
Password	
Security	
Website	
Username	
Email	
Password	
Security	

A

Website	
Username	
Email	
Password	
Security	
Website	
Username	
Email	
Password	
Security	
Website	
Username	
Email	
Password	
Security	

A

Website	
Username	
Email	
Password	
Security	
Website	
Username	
Email	
Password	
Security	
Website	
Username	
Email	
Password	
Security	

A

Website	
Username	
Email	
Password	
Security	
Website	
Username	
Email	
Password	
Security	
Website	
Username	
Email	
Password	
Security	

B

Website	
Username	
Email	
Password	
Security	
Website	
Username	
Email	
Password	
Security	
Website	
Username	
Email	
Password	
Security	

B

Website	
Username	
Email	
Password	
Security	
Website	
Username	
Email	
Password	
Security	
Website	
Username	
Email	
Password	
Security	

B

Website	
Username	
Email	
Password	
Security	
Website	
Username	
Email	
Password	
Security	
Website	
Username	
Email	
Password	
Security	

B

Website	
Username	
Email	
Password	
Security	
Website	
Username	
Email	
Password	
Security	
Website	
Username	
Email	
Password	
Security	

B

Website	
Username	
Email	
Password	
Security	
Website	
Username	
Email	
Password	
Security	
Website	
Username	
Email	
Password	
Security	

B

Website	
Username	
Email	
Password	
Security	
Website	
Username	
Email	
Password	
Security	
Website	
Username	
Email	
Password	
Security	

Website	
Username	
Email	
Password	
Security	
Website	
Username	
Email	
Password	
Security	
Website	
Username	
Email	
Password	
Security	

C

Website	
Username	
Email	
Password	
Security	
Website	
Username	
Email	
Password	
Security	
Website	
Username	
Email	
Password	
Security	

Website	
Username	
Email	
Password	
Security	
Website	
Username	
Email	
Password	
Security	
Website	
Username	
Email	
Password	
Security	

C

Website	
Username	
Email	
Password	
Security	
Website	
Username	
Email	
Password	
Security	
Website	
Username	
Email	
Password	
Security	

Website	
Username	
Email	
Password	
Security	
Website	
Username	
Email	
Password	
Security	
Website	
Username	
Email	
Password	
Security	

C

Website	
Username	
Email	
Password	
Security	
Website	
Username	
Email	
Password	
Security	
Website	
Username	
Email	
Password	
Security	

D

C-D

Website	
Username	
Email	
Password	
Security	
Website	
Username	
Email	
Password	
Security	
Website	
Username	
Email	
Password	
Security	

D

Website	
Username	
Email	
Password	
Security	
Website	
Username	
Email	
Password	
Security	
Website	
Username	
Email	
Password	
Security	

D

Website	
Username	
Email	
Password	
Security	
Website	
Username	
Email	
Password	
Security	
Website	
Username	
Email	
Password	
Security	

D

Website	
Username	
Email	
Password	
Security	
Website	
Username	
Email	
Password	
Security	
Website	
Username	
Email	
Password	
Security	

D

C-D

Website	
Username	
Email	
Password	
Security	
Website	
Username	
Email	
Password	
Security	
Website	
Username	
Email	
Password	
Security	

D

Website	
Username	
Email	
Password	
Security	
Website	
Username	
Email	
Password	
Security	
Website	
Username	
Email	
Password	
Security	

Website	
Username	
Email	
Password	
Security	
Website	
Username	
Email	
Password	
Security	
Website	
Username	
Email	
Password	
Security	

E

Website	
Username	
Email	
Password	
Security	
Website	
Username	
Email	
Password	
Security	
Website	
Username	
Email	
Password	
Security	

E

E-F

Website	
Username	
Email	
Password	
Security	
Website	
Username	
Email	
Password	
Security	
Website	
Username	
Email	
Password	
Security	

E

Website	
Username	
Email	
Password	
Security	
Website	
Username	
Email	
Password	
Security	
Website	
Username	
Email	
Password	
Security	

E

E-F

Website	
Username	
Email	
Password	
Security	
Website	
Username	
Email	
Password	
Security	
Website	
Username	
Email	
Password	
Security	

E

Website	
Username	
Email	
Password	
Security	
Website	
Username	
Email	
Password	
Security	
Website	
Username	
Email	
Password	
Security	

F

Website	
Username	
Email	
Password	
Security	
Website	
Username	
Email	
Password	
Security	
Website	
Username	
Email	
Password	
Security	

F

Website	
Username	
Email	
Password	
Security	
Website	
Username	
Email	
Password	
Security	
Website	
Username	
Email	
Password	
Security	

F

Website	
Username	
Email	
Password	
Security	
Website	
Username	
Email	
Password	
Security	
Website	
Username	
Email	
Password	
Security	

F

Website	
Username	
Email	
Password	
Security	
Website	
Username	
Email	
Password	
Security	
Website	
Username	
Email	
Password	
Security	

F

Website	
Username	
Email	
Password	
Security	
Website	
Username	
Email	
Password	
Security	
Website	
Username	
Email	
Password	
Security	

E-F

F

Website	
Username	
Email	
Password	
Security	
Website	
Username	
Email	
Password	
Security	
Website	
Username	
Email	
Password	
Security	

G

Website	
Username	
Email	
Password	
Security	
Website	
Username	
Email	
Password	
Security	
Website	
Username	
Email	
Password	
Security	

G

Website	
Username	
Email	
Password	
Security	
Website	
Username	
Email	
Password	
Security	
Website	
Username	
Email	
Password	
Security	

G

Website	
Username	
Email	
Password	
Security	
Website	
Username	
Email	
Password	
Security	
Website	
Username	
Email	
Password	
Security	

G-H

G

Website	
Username	
Email	
Password	
Security	
Website	
Username	
Email	
Password	
Security	
Website	
Username	
Email	
Password	
Security	

Website	
Username	
Email	
Password	
Security	
Website	
Username	
Email	
Password	
Security	
Website	
Username	
Email	
Password	
Security	

G

Website	
Username	
Email	
Password	
Security	
Website	
Username	
Email	
Password	
Security	
Website	
Username	
Email	
Password	
Security	

H

Website	
Username	
Email	
Password	
Security	
Website	
Username	
Email	
Password	
Security	
Website	
Username	
Email	
Password	
Security	

H

Website	
Username	
Email	
Password	
Security	
Website	
Username	
Email	
Password	
Security	
Website	
Username	
Email	
Password	
Security	

H

Website	
Username	
Email	
Password	
Security	
Website	
Username	
Email	
Password	
Security	
Website	
Username	
Email	
Password	
Security	

G-H

H

Website	
Username	
Email	
Password	
Security	
Website	
Username	
Email	
Password	
Security	
Website	
Username	
Email	
Password	
Security	

H

Website	
Username	
Email	
Password	
Security	
Website	
Username	
Email	
Password	
Security	
Website	
Username	
Email	
Password	
Security	

H

Website	
Username	
Email	
Password	
Security	
Website	
Username	
Email	
Password	
Security	
Website	
Username	
Email	
Password	
Security	

I

Website	
Username	
Email	
Password	
Security	
Website	
Username	
Email	
Password	
Security	
Website	
Username	
Email	
Password	
Security	

I-J

I

Website	
Username	
Email	
Password	
Security	
Website	
Username	
Email	
Password	
Security	
Website	
Username	
Email	
Password	
Security	

Website	
Username	
Email	
Password	
Security	
Website	
Username	
Email	
Password	
Security	
Website	
Username	
Email	
Password	
Security	

I

Website	
Username	
Email	
Password	
Security	
Website	
Username	
Email	
Password	
Security	
Website	
Username	
Email	
Password	
Security	

Website	
Username	
Email	
Password	
Security	
Website	
Username	
Email	
Password	
Security	
Website	
Username	
Email	
Password	
Security	

I

Website	
Username	
Email	
Password	
Security	
Website	
Username	
Email	
Password	
Security	
Website	
Username	
Email	
Password	
Security	

J

Website	
Username	
Email	
Password	
Security	
Website	
Username	
Email	
Password	
Security	
Website	
Username	
Email	
Password	
Security	

I-J

J

Website	
Username	
Email	
Password	
Security	
Website	
Username	
Email	
Password	
Security	
Website	
Username	
Email	
Password	
Security	

J

Website	
Username	
Email	
Password	
Security	
Website	
Username	
Email	
Password	
Security	
Website	
Username	
Email	
Password	
Security	

J

Website	
Username	
Email	
Password	
Security	
Website	
Username	
Email	
Password	
Security	
Website	
Username	
Email	
Password	
Security	

J

Website	
Username	
Email	
Password	
Security	
Website	
Username	
Email	
Password	
Security	
Website	
Username	
Email	
Password	
Security	

J

Website	
Username	
Email	
Password	
Security	
Website	
Username	
Email	
Password	
Security	
Website	
Username	
Email	
Password	
Security	

K

Website	
Username	
Email	
Password	
Security	
Website	
Username	
Email	
Password	
Security	
Website	
Username	
Email	
Password	
Security	

K

Website	
Username	
Email	
Password	
Security	
Website	
Username	
Email	
Password	
Security	
Website	
Username	
Email	
Password	
Security	

K

Website	
Username	
Email	
Password	
Security	
Website	
Username	
Email	
Password	
Security	
Website	
Username	
Email	
Password	
Security	

K-L

K

Website	
Username	
Email	
Password	
Security	
Website	
Username	
Email	
Password	
Security	
Website	
Username	
Email	
Password	
Security	

K

Website	
Username	
Email	
Password	
Security	
Website	
Username	
Email	
Password	
Security	
Website	
Username	
Email	
Password	
Security	

K

Website	
Username	
Email	
Password	
Security	
Website	
Username	
Email	
Password	
Security	
Website	
Username	
Email	
Password	
Security	

L

Website	
Username	
Email	
Password	
Security	
Website	
Username	
Email	
Password	
Security	
Website	
Username	
Email	
Password	
Security	

L

Website	
Username	
Email	
Password	
Security	
Website	
Username	
Email	
Password	
Security	
Website	
Username	
Email	
Password	
Security	

L

Website	
Username	
Email	
Password	
Security	
Website	
Username	
Email	
Password	
Security	
Website	
Username	
Email	
Password	
Security	

L

Website	
Username	
Email	
Password	
Security	
Website	
Username	
Email	
Password	
Security	
Website	
Username	
Email	
Password	
Security	

Website	
Username	
Email	
Password	
Security	
Website	
Username	
Email	
Password	
Security	
Website	
Username	
Email	
Password	
Security	

L

Website	
Username	
Email	
Password	
Security	
Website	
Username	
Email	
Password	
Security	
Website	
Username	
Email	
Password	
Security	

M

Website	
Username	
Email	
Password	
Security	
Website	
Username	
Email	
Password	
Security	
Website	
Username	
Email	
Password	
Security	

M-N

M

Website	
Username	
Email	
Password	
Security	
Website	
Username	
Email	
Password	
Security	
Website	
Username	
Email	
Password	
Security	

Website	
Username	
Email	
Password	
Security	
Website	
Username	
Email	
Password	
Security	
Website	
Username	
Email	
Password	
Security	

M

Website	
Username	
Email	
Password	
Security	
Website	
Username	
Email	
Password	
Security	
Website	
Username	
Email	
Password	
Security	

M

Website	
Username	
Email	
Password	
Security	
Website	
Username	
Email	
Password	
Security	
Website	
Username	
Email	
Password	
Security	

M

Website	
Username	
Email	
Password	
Security	
Website	
Username	
Email	
Password	
Security	
Website	
Username	
Email	
Password	
Security	

Website	
Username	
Email	
Password	
Security	
Website	
Username	
Email	
Password	
Security	
Website	
Username	
Email	
Password	
Security	

N

Website	
Username	
Email	
Password	
Security	
Website	
Username	
Email	
Password	
Security	
Website	
Username	
Email	
Password	
Security	

N

Website	
Username	
Email	
Password	
Security	
Website	
Username	
Email	
Password	
Security	
Website	
Username	
Email	
Password	
Security	

N

Website	
Username	
Email	
Password	
Security	
Website	
Username	
Email	
Password	
Security	
Website	
Username	
Email	
Password	
Security	

N

Website	
Username	
Email	
Password	
Security	
Website	
Username	
Email	
Password	
Security	
Website	
Username	
Email	
Password	
Security	

M-N

N

Website	
Username	
Email	
Password	
Security	
Website	
Username	
Email	
Password	
Security	
Website	
Username	
Email	
Password	
Security	

Website	
Username	
Email	
Password	
Security	
Website	
Username	
Email	
Password	
Security	
Website	
Username	
Email	
Password	
Security	

O

Website	
Username	
Email	
Password	
Security	
Website	
Username	
Email	
Password	
Security	
Website	
Username	
Email	
Password	
Security	

O

Website	
Username	
Email	
Password	
Security	
Website	
Username	
Email	
Password	
Security	
Website	
Username	
Email	
Password	
Security	

O-P

O

Website	
Username	
Email	
Password	
Security	
Website	
Username	
Email	
Password	
Security	
Website	
Username	
Email	
Password	
Security	

O

Website	
Username	
Email	
Password	
Security	
Website	
Username	
Email	
Password	
Security	
Website	
Username	
Email	
Password	
Security	

O

Website	
Username	
Email	
Password	
Security	
Website	
Username	
Email	
Password	
Security	
Website	
Username	
Email	
Password	
Security	

P

Website	
Username	
Email	
Password	
Security	
Website	
Username	
Email	
Password	
Security	
Website	
Username	
Email	
Password	
Security	

P

Website	
Username	
Email	
Password	
Security	
Website	
Username	
Email	
Password	
Security	
Website	
Username	
Email	
Password	
Security	

P

Website	
Username	
Email	
Password	
Security	
Website	
Username	
Email	
Password	
Security	
Website	
Username	
Email	
Password	
Security	

O-P

P

Website	
Username	
Email	
Password	
Security	
Website	
Username	
Email	
Password	
Security	
Website	
Username	
Email	
Password	
Security	

P

Website	
Username	
Email	
Password	
Security	
Website	
Username	
Email	
Password	
Security	
Website	
Username	
Email	
Password	
Security	

O-P

P

Website	
Username	
Email	
Password	
Security	
Website	
Username	
Email	
Password	
Security	
Website	
Username	
Email	
Password	
Security	

Q

Website	
Username	
Email	
Password	
Security	
Website	
Username	
Email	
Password	
Security	
Website	
Username	
Email	
Password	
Security	

Q

Website	
Username	
Email	
Password	
Security	
Website	
Username	
Email	
Password	
Security	
Website	
Username	
Email	
Password	
Security	

Q

Website	
Username	
Email	
Password	
Security	
Website	
Username	
Email	
Password	
Security	
Website	
Username	
Email	
Password	
Security	

Q

Website	
Username	
Email	
Password	
Security	
Website	
Username	
Email	
Password	
Security	
Website	
Username	
Email	
Password	
Security	

Q

Website	
Username	
Email	
Password	
Security	
Website	
Username	
Email	
Password	
Security	
Website	
Username	
Email	
Password	
Security	

Q

Website	
Username	
Email	
Password	
Security	
Website	
Username	
Email	
Password	
Security	
Website	
Username	
Email	
Password	
Security	

R

Website	
Username	
Email	
Password	
Security	
Website	
Username	
Email	
Password	
Security	
Website	
Username	
Email	
Password	
Security	

R

Website	
Username	
Email	
Password	
Security	
Website	
Username	
Email	
Password	
Security	
Website	
Username	
Email	
Password	
Security	

R

Website	
Username	
Email	
Password	
Security	
Website	
Username	
Email	
Password	
Security	
Website	
Username	
Email	
Password	
Security	

Q-R

R

Website	
Username	
Email	
Password	
Security	
Website	
Username	
Email	
Password	
Security	
Website	
Username	
Email	
Password	
Security	

R

Website	
Username	
Email	
Password	
Security	
Website	
Username	
Email	
Password	
Security	
Website	
Username	
Email	
Password	
Security	

Q-R

R

Website	
Username	
Email	
Password	
Security	
Website	
Username	
Email	
Password	
Security	
Website	
Username	
Email	
Password	
Security	

S

Website	
Username	
Email	
Password	
Security	
Website	
Username	
Email	
Password	
Security	
Website	
Username	
Email	
Password	
Security	

S-T

S

Website	
Username	
Email	
Password	
Security	
Website	
Username	
Email	
Password	
Security	
Website	
Username	
Email	
Password	
Security	

S

Website	
Username	
Email	
Password	
Security	
Website	
Username	
Email	
Password	
Security	
Website	
Username	
Email	
Password	
Security	

S-T

S

Website	
Username	
Email	
Password	
Security	
Website	
Username	
Email	
Password	
Security	
Website	
Username	
Email	
Password	
Security	

Website	
Username	
Email	
Password	
Security	
Website	
Username	
Email	
Password	
Security	
Website	
Username	
Email	
Password	
Security	

S

Website	
Username	
Email	
Password	
Security	
Website	
Username	
Email	
Password	
Security	
Website	
Username	
Email	
Password	
Security	

T

Website	
Username	
Email	
Password	
Security	
Website	
Username	
Email	
Password	
Security	
Website	
Username	
Email	
Password	
Security	

T

Website	
Username	
Email	
Password	
Security	
Website	
Username	
Email	
Password	
Security	
Website	
Username	
Email	
Password	
Security	

T

Website	
Username	
Email	
Password	
Security	
Website	
Username	
Email	
Password	
Security	
Website	
Username	
Email	
Password	
Security	

S-T

T

Website	
Username	
Email	
Password	
Security	
Website	
Username	
Email	
Password	
Security	
Website	
Username	
Email	
Password	
Security	

T

Website	
Username	
Email	
Password	
Security	
Website	
Username	
Email	
Password	
Security	
Website	
Username	
Email	
Password	
Security	

T

Website	
Username	
Email	
Password	
Security	
Website	
Username	
Email	
Password	
Security	
Website	
Username	
Email	
Password	
Security	

U

Website	
Username	
Email	
Password	
Security	
Website	
Username	
Email	
Password	
Security	
Website	
Username	
Email	
Password	
Security	

U

Website	
Username	
Email	
Password	
Security	
Website	
Username	
Email	
Password	
Security	
Website	
Username	
Email	
Password	
Security	

U

Website	
Username	
Email	
Password	
Security	
Website	
Username	
Email	
Password	
Security	
Website	
Username	
Email	
Password	
Security	

U

Website	
Username	
Email	
Password	
Security	
Website	
Username	
Email	
Password	
Security	
Website	
Username	
Email	
Password	
Security	

U

Website	
Username	
Email	
Password	
Security	
Website	
Username	
Email	
Password	
Security	
Website	
Username	
Email	
Password	
Security	

U

Website	
Username	
Email	
Password	
Security	
Website	
Username	
Email	
Password	
Security	
Website	
Username	
Email	
Password	
Security	

V

Website	
Username	
Email	
Password	
Security	
Website	
Username	
Email	
Password	
Security	
Website	
Username	
Email	
Password	
Security	

V

Website	
Username	
Email	
Password	
Security	
Website	
Username	
Email	
Password	
Security	
Website	
Username	
Email	
Password	
Security	

V

Website	
Username	
Email	
Password	
Security	
Website	
Username	
Email	
Password	
Security	
Website	
Username	
Email	
Password	
Security	

U-V

V

Website	
Username	
Email	
Password	
Security	
Website	
Username	
Email	
Password	
Security	
Website	
Username	
Email	
Password	
Security	

V

Website	
Username	
Email	
Password	
Security	
Website	
Username	
Email	
Password	
Security	
Website	
Username	
Email	
Password	
Security	

V

Website	
Username	
Email	
Password	
Security	
Website	
Username	
Email	
Password	
Security	
Website	
Username	
Email	
Password	
Security	

W

Website	
Username	
Email	
Password	
Security	
Website	
Username	
Email	
Password	
Security	
Website	
Username	
Email	
Password	
Security	

W

Website	
Username	
Email	
Password	
Security	
Website	
Username	
Email	
Password	
Security	
Website	
Username	
Email	
Password	
Security	

W

Website	
Username	
Email	
Password	
Security	
Website	
Username	
Email	
Password	
Security	
Website	
Username	
Email	
Password	
Security	

W-X

W

Website	
Username	
Email	
Password	
Security	
Website	
Username	
Email	
Password	
Security	
Website	
Username	
Email	
Password	
Security	

W

Website	
Username	
Email	
Password	
Security	
Website	
Username	
Email	
Password	
Security	
Website	
Username	
Email	
Password	
Security	

W

Website	
Username	
Email	
Password	
Security	
Website	
Username	
Email	
Password	
Security	
Website	
Username	
Email	
Password	
Security	

X

Website	
Username	
Email	
Password	
Security	
Website	
Username	
Email	
Password	
Security	
Website	
Username	
Email	
Password	
Security	

X

Website	
Username	
Email	
Password	
Security	
Website	
Username	
Email	
Password	
Security	
Website	
Username	
Email	
Password	
Security	

X

Website	
Username	
Email	
Password	
Security	
Website	
Username	
Email	
Password	
Security	
Website	
Username	
Email	
Password	
Security	

W-X

X

Website	
Username	
Email	
Password	
Security	
Website	
Username	
Email	
Password	
Security	
Website	
Username	
Email	
Password	
Security	

X

Website	
Username	
Email	
Password	
Security	
Website	
Username	
Email	
Password	
Security	
Website	
Username	
Email	
Password	
Security	

X

Website	
Username	
Email	
Password	
Security	
Website	
Username	
Email	
Password	
Security	
Website	
Username	
Email	
Password	
Security	

Y

Website	
Username	
Email	
Password	
Security	
Website	
Username	
Email	
Password	
Security	
Website	
Username	
Email	
Password	
Security	

Y

Website	
Username	
Email	
Password	
Security	
Website	
Username	
Email	
Password	
Security	
Website	
Username	
Email	
Password	
Security	

Y

Website	
Username	
Email	
Password	
Security	
Website	
Username	
Email	
Password	
Security	
Website	
Username	
Email	
Password	
Security	

Y

Website	
Username	
Email	
Password	
Security	
Website	
Username	
Email	
Password	
Security	
Website	
Username	
Email	
Password	
Security	

Y

Website	
Username	
Email	
Password	
Security	
Website	
Username	
Email	
Password	
Security	
Website	
Username	
Email	
Password	
Security	

Y

Website	
Username	
Email	
Password	
Security	
Website	
Username	
Email	
Password	
Security	
Website	
Username	
Email	
Password	
Security	

Z

Website	
Username	
Email	
Password	
Security	
Website	
Username	
Email	
Password	
Security	
Website	
Username	
Email	
Password	
Security	

Z

Website	
Username	
Email	
Password	
Security	
Website	
Username	
Email	
Password	
Security	
Website	
Username	
Email	
Password	
Security	

Z

Website	
Username	
Email	
Password	
Security	
Website	
Username	
Email	
Password	
Security	
Website	
Username	
Email	
Password	
Security	

Z

Website	
Username	
Email	
Password	
Security	
Website	
Username	
Email	
Password	
Security	
Website	
Username	
Email	
Password	
Security	

Z

Website	
Username	
Email	
Password	
Security	
Website	
Username	
Email	
Password	
Security	
Website	
Username	
Email	
Password	
Security	

Z

Website	
Username	
Email	
Password	
Security	
Website	
Username	
Email	
Password	
Security	
Website	
Username	
Email	
Password	
Security	

Website	
Username	
Email	
Password	
Security	
Website	
Username	
Email	
Password	
Security	
Website	
Username	
Email	
Password	
Security	

0-9

Website	
Username	
Email	
Password	
Security	
Website	
Username	
Email	
Password	
Security	
Website	
Username	
Email	
Password	
Security	

0-9

Website	
Username	
Email	
Password	
Security	
Website	
Username	
Email	
Password	
Security	
Website	
Username	
Email	
Password	
Security	

0-9

Website	
Username	
Email	
Password	
Security	
Website	
Username	
Email	
Password	
Security	
Website	
Username	
Email	
Password	
Security	

0-9

Website	
Username	
Email	
Password	
Security	
Website	
Username	
Email	
Password	
Security	
Website	
Username	
Email	
Password	
Security	

Personal

Name	
Address	
City	
Province	
Postal Code	
Telephone	
Mobile	
Email	
Password	
Bank	
Account	
Credit Card	
Expiry	
Security	

Made in the USA
Middletown, DE
05 November 2026

36544997R10093